LIVING THE HYGGE LIFESTYLE

How to Use the Danish Art of Hygge to Build

a Comfortable, Peaceful, and Happy Life

Contents

Introduction

Are you so stressed that you think you're losing it? Do you feel like you're working too much? Are you always cranky? Do you feel too tired? If yes, you need to the art of slowing down and cozying up. It's called Hygge and it's getting more and more popular in the Western World.

Hygge (pronounced as hue-gah) is the Danish art of living a cozy and happy life. It is the light that illuminates the soul. It is the reason why Danish people stay happy even during the coldest and darkest day.

Hygge helps you slow down and enjoy the simple things in life. It helps you see things in rose-colored glasses. It cultivates gratitude and joy. It helps you connect with the people around you and build meaningful relationships.

This Danish custom is about being consciously cozy. It is also the pursuit of everyday pleasure and happiness. It is about being with the people you love. It's about indulgence and enjoying the beautiful things this life has to offer. It's about cozying up during cold winter days, but it's also about discovering the beauty of the outdoors.

Many people use the Danish concept of hygge to cozy up during cold winter days. But, hygge is not just something you practice during the winter season. It's something that you can do all year round.

In this book, you'll learn what hygge is and how you can use to build a happier and stress-free life.

In this book, you'll learn:

- What hygge is and where it came from
- The basic principles of hygge
- How to adopt the hygge mindset
- How to turn your home into a hygge paradise
- How to practice hygge in your workplace
- Cozy hygge recipes for every season
- How to practice hygge during autumn, winter, spring, and summer
- How to start your hygge practice with a 15 day challenge

- Simple hygge tips and strategies that you can use to be happier and live a more comfortable life

- And more!

It's time to stop sleepwalking through life. It's time to live in the present moment and really enjoy everything life has to offer. It's time to connect with others and make time for things that truly matter. Now is the perfect time to give hygge a try and see how it magically transforms your life.

Thank you for downloading this book and I hope that you enjoy it!

CHAPTER- 1

The Origin of Hygge: Where Does it Come From?

Denmark is not only known for its breathtaking views and great government. It's also considered as one of the happiest countries of the world. Hygge is often credited as the reason that Denmark is one of the top five countries in the World Happiness Report year after year.

Hygge was shortlisted as the word of the year in 2016. Since then, it is slowly finding its place in the United States.

In Denmark, hygge is used both as an adjective and a noun. But, it's more of a way of life. It is also a psychological state. It's the state of being cozy and safe.

Hygge is a Danish way of life. But, it has German origins. This term is very much like the German concept of gemutlichkeit, which means cordiality and friendliness.

There's no exact English translation for hygge, but it means "to give happiness, comfort, joy, and courage". It was derived from an Old Norse (North Germanic Language) word called "hyggja", which means "being happy about something". A number of historians believe that hygge was derived from another Old Norse word called "hugr", which means to embrace and show love. Hugr is now known as "hug", the art of holding someone you care about close to your body.

Hygge has become synonymous to Danish culture. But, did you know that hygge did not originate in Denmark? This art of living the good life was actually conceived in Norway in the late 18th century, but soon became popular in Denmark.

This Nordic lifestyle first appeared in Danish texts in the early 19th century. It has become a huge part of the Danish culture.

Although hygge has a strong Danish origin, it's not something that you can only practice in Denmark. In fact, it's something that you can practice in every part of the world, even in places with tropical climates.

Hygge came a long way from being a small Danish custom to being a global phenomenon.

CHAPTER- 2

What is Hygge and How Do I Start?

Hygge is now practiced globally, but, it's just as Danish as the sweet æbleskiver . It's the art of living a cozy life. It is about creating a nice, homey, and cozy atmosphere. It is about being connected with other people. It is about surrounding yourself with beautiful things. It's about sitting next to the fireplace and reading a good book. It's also about indulgence and finding joy in simple things.

For many Westeners, hygge is about candles, sinful comfort food, delicious drinks, cozy socks, soft blankets, and dinner parties with family and friends. But, hygge is more than that. It is about being present. It is about truly connecting to other people. It's about building happy relationships. It is about self-care and indulging mindfully. It is about covering yourself up with soft blankets during winter time, but it's also about enjoying the great outdoors during summer time.

To sum it all up, hygge is about finding happiness in simple things. It's about appreciating life. It's about allowing yourself to indulge every now and it. It's about living your life to the fullest.

How to Start Your Hygge Journey

The art of living a cozy life is not as hard as you think. Here's how you can start practicing hygge and feel happier:

Step 1: Adopt the Hygge Mindset

Hygge is not just about drinking hot chocolate or lighting scented candles. It is a state of mind. It's about choosing to see the good in every situation. It is about choosing to celebrate the little things in life. We'll discuss this in detail in the next chapter.

Step 2: Turn your Home into a Hygge Paradise

Surround yourself with things that spark joy in your heart. Make your home as comfortable as you can. Heat your home up with candles during cold winter nights. Make sure to open your windows and let the light in during summer days. We will discuss this in detail later in a book.

Step 3: Learn to Appreciate the Little Things in Life

Gratitude is the foundation of happiness. You don't have to accumulate a lot of things to be happy. You just have to appreciate what you have. Be grateful for all the blessings you have received over the years. You're more blessed than you think, so start looking at the world with "gratitude lenses".

Walk around your neighborhood and appreciate how beautiful it is. Look around you and realize how lucky you are to enjoy that beautiful view. Do something you like to do like painting flower pots or yoga. Look at the sunset and enjoy its captivating colors. Take time to smell the flowers.

Step 4: Indulge in Good Food

Hygge is about enjoying the little pleasures of life – the sunsets, bubble baths, good book, and delicious food. Don't deprive yourself. Eat a slice of chocolate mousse or a cup of sinful mac and cheese. Eat food that makes you feel cozy and happy.

Step 5: Spend Time with People Who Are Important to You

Hygge is also called "socializing for introverts". It's about enjoying good food with the people you love. To practice hygge, turn your phone off when you're having dinner with your family. Be present. Appreciate every moment with the people close to your heart.

Hygge is about connecting to other human beings. But, you don't have to be an introvert to practice this Danish lifestyle. All you have to do is to create happy memories with the people you care about. Go on a coffee date with your friends. Host a dinner party or a movie viewing party with your favorite people. Cuddle with your spouse or partner. Play with your kids and have after-work drinks with your colleagues.

You have to realize that human connection is one of the most important components of happiness. So, stop staring at your phone or computer screen and start spending time with people you like and respect.

Starting your hygge journey is not as hard as you think. In chapter 10 of this book, you'll find a 15 day challenge that will help you start living the "hygge" lifestyle.

CHAPTER- 3

The Hygge State of Mind: How to Have the Hygge Mindset

Hygge is getting more and more popular in the West as a lifestyle trend. But, it's not just a shopping list or a décor trend. It is a way of life. It is a mindset.

Hygge is about having a warm candle-lit dinner with your friends. It is about cuddling with your loved one in a cozy blanket. It is about sitting on your porch and watching the sun rise. It is more than just an explosive sensory experience. It goes beyond cosiness and comfort. Hygge is also the art of appreciating the beauty of all simple things. It's about living with a grateful heart. Below are some tips that you can use to achieve "hygge state of mind".

Choose to See the Positive

Denmark is a beautiful country. It's filled with pastel-colored buildings. It has wonderful beaches, fascinating cityscapes, and breathtaking landscapes. It's glorious during the summertime. But, it can get too cold during the winter time. But, the Danish people choose to get the best out of the wintertime by practicing hygge.

You see, hygge is not just about being cozy or comfortable. It is also about adopting a positive mindset. It's about choosing to see the positive in every bad situation. It's about being a half-glass full kind of guy.

Slow Down

We live in a fast-paced world. We multi-task, we eat fast food, and we are relentless in pursuing our goals. No wonder that a lot of us are anxious and depressed.

Hygge is the art of slowing down and living in the present moment. It is the art of creating amazing memories with your loved ones. It is about taking your time.

Here's what you can do to slow down:

1. Do less.

Don't feel guilty about doing less. Weed out activities that are not aligned with your goals. Don't get lost in meaningless busyness. Focus on activities that bring you joy, the ones that make your heart leap.

2. Rest when you have to.

All work and no play make your life unbalanced. So, do yourself a favor – take a break. Rest when you're tired.

Resting strengthens your immune system. It energizes you and improves your health. It also slows down the aging process and it increases your efficiency and creativity.

3. Do digital detox every now and then.

Electronic devices help us communicate with our loved ones, even when they are away. But, these devices are sometimes distracting and can reduce your productivity. So, turn off your phone when you're doing something important so you could focus.

Spend a weekend with your loved one. Turn your phone off and just enjoy your time together. Don't take phone calls. Don't post anything on Instagram. Don't check your Facebook.

4. Connect with nature.

There's something about nature that's just so captivating. It revitalizes your spirit. Instead of going to the gym, go hiking instead and take time to appreciate the wonders and beauty of nature.

5. Don't multi-task.

A lot of people think that multi-tasking is the key to increasing productivity. It's true to some extent. But, multi-tasking can sometimes slow you down and can take away your focus and mental clarity. To live a peaceful life, do one thing at a time.

6. Drive slower.

Driving slow is safer and it also gives you an opportunity to enjoy your ride. It's an opportunity to really appreciate the views of your city.

Lastly, take a mental day off at least once a month. Whenever you feel tired, too stressed, or you feel like you're about to break down, just take a day off. Watch a movie, read a book, or drive to the nearest beach.

Connect with Your Tribe

Hygge can be about reading a book and enjoy your "alone time" in a cozy café. But, it is ultimately about making time for your tribe – the people you care about.

Have a dinner date with your friends. Host a game night. Be there when a friend needs you. Don't be afraid to show your affection. You have to smile, hug, and kiss more often.

Surround yourself with people who believe in you and let go of all those who are trying to bring you down.

Feel the Joie de Vivre

Joie de Vivre is a French concept that literally means "joy of life". It's that enthusiasm and excitement about life. It is the art of living passionately. It is about enjoying every moment of your life.

Here's how you can experience joie de vivre:

1. Travel.

Don't be afraid to go outside your zip code. Save a portion of your income each and travel to a place you've never been before at least twice a year. Travel to a different country and enjoy other people's culture.

2. Dance like no one is watching.

Dancing makes you feel alive. It's a celebration of what your body can do. Put your headphones on and dance while you're washing the dishes or doing the laundry.

3. Go outside.

It's tempting to just stay at home all day. But, to truly live life, you must go outside and do exciting things. You can go hiking and camping. You can do rock climbing, surfing, skiing, and rock climbing.

4. Enjoy good food.

Life is short, so soak in all the flavors and pleasure this world has to offer. Cook food that makes you happy. Eat in your favorite restaurant and hang out in your favorite coffee shop.

You only have one life, so enjoy it. Make the most out of it.

Gratitude: The Gateway to Contentment

Gratitude has a transformative power. It can make you happier and more compassionate. It can make you more content and satisfied, too. It creates a cocktail of positive emotions and it helps reduce negative feelings such as anger, sadness, depression, anxiety, resentment, and guilt.

Gratitude is not only the gateway to contentment. It's also a key to happiness. Here are a few tips that you can use to maintain the attitude of gratitude.

1. Realize that you are blessed.

No matter what your life is like right now, there's someone out there who will give everything for what you have. If you have a job, a car, a roof over your head, and a few hundred dollars in your bank account, you are more blessed than you think.

2. Write down the things that you are grateful for.

Buy a notebook and call it your "gratitude journal". Every morning when you wake up, write down all the things that you are grateful for. It may be your job, your parents, your home, your neighborhood, or the food in your table.

3. Express your gratitude to the people around you.

Take time to appreciate the people around you. Say "thank you" to a barista serving you coffee or to your Uber driver. Say "thank you" to your spouse for everything that he/she does for you. Expressing gratitude to the people around you doesn't only make you likeable. It makes you happier, too.

Gratitude rewires your body. It decreases your pain and helps relieve your stress. It increases your vitality and energy. It makes you more resilient, allowing you to bounce back and easily recover from setbacks.

CHAPTER- 4

How to Practice Hygge at Home and at Work

If you type in "hygge" on Instagram, you'll find pictures of blankets, flowers, books, throw pillows, candles, hot chocolate, and beautiful living rooms.

Yes, hygge is about being grateful and being connected to the people around you. It's about doing something that makes you happy. But it's also about making your home and workplace more comfortable. It's about candles and attractive throw pillows. It's about neutral colors.

Here's how you can practice hygge at work and at home:

Decorate Your Home with Scented Candles

Tealight candles add warmth in your home and they are affordable, too. They create an ambience of comfort and relaxation. You can try different scents, such as rose, ylang

ylang, lemon, chamomile, cinnamon, vanilla, lavender, orange, and goji berry.

Place Soft Blankets Around Your Home

Blankets are not only for the bedroom. You can also place it on your couch or even on your porch furniture.

Decorate Your Sofa and Bed with Soft and stylish Throw Pillows

Throw pillows are easy on the eyes. They are cute, cheap, and they're cozy, too. They make your home more comfortable.

Invest in a Good Faux Fur

Faux fur can make your home look like a million bucks. They're fluffy and comfortable.

Create a Hygge Corner or a Book Nook

Creating a book nook is an important part of hygge. This is the place where you sit, enjoy a cup of hot chocolate, and read your favorite book.

Make sure that this corner is near your fireplace and has a comfortable cushioned chair, a small bookshelf filled with your favorite book, and a small table where you can write on your journal. You can also decorate it with twinkly lights.

Make Your Bathroom Look Like A Spa

Decorate your bathroom with candles, flowers, and fluffy towels. Make it a place where you can relax. Spray a little bit of lavender scent around your bathroom.

Use Neutral Colors

Neutral colors are more relaxing and easy on the eyes. But, this doesn't mean that you can't place colorful conversation pieces.

Invest in Good Lamps

Good lighting makes your home warmer. So, don't be afraid to spend a little bit of money on high quality lighting.

Place Fresh Flowers and Scented Candles on Your Work Desk

Scented décor and fresh flowers can lighten up your office. You can also decorate your workplace with string lights if your office allows it.

Bring a Mug at Work

Having a warm beverage makes you feel warm and at home, even when you're at work.

Keep Your Workplace Clean at All Times

You can't think clearly if you're surrounded with clutter. So, make sure that you keep your workplace clean all the time.

Like it or not, you're most likely to spend most of your time either at your work or in your home. So, you must make an effort to create a cozy ambience both in your home and work.

CHAPTER- 5

The Hygge Lifestyle

Hygge is about being happy, taking care of yourself, and enjoying life's simple joys. It is a way of life. It's about harmony, togetherness, simplicity, and contentment. Hygge is being happy and comfortable. It is sharing a meal with loved one. It is laughter, joy, gratitude, and contentment.

Spend A Few More Minutes in Bed

Many self-help experts would tell you to get up right after your alarm goes off. But, hygge is about being comfortable and enjoying the little things in life. So, don't be afraid to spend a few more minutes in bed.

Do Digital Detox Every Now And Then

Social media has taken over our lives and it's making a lot of us unhappy. So, to restore balance in your life, you have to go digital detox every now and then. Take a few days off from social media and enjoy the great outdoors.

Be present. Turn off your phone (or the TV) when you're having dinner with your loved ones so you can really have a great conversation with them.

Hug Your Loved Ones Often

Tomorrow is uncertain for us human beings, so hug your loved ones while you still can. Let them know how you feel about them and how they make you happy. Invite them into your home and cook delicious meals for them. Let them know how much you appreciate them.

Host a Potluck Dinner with Your Colleagues

You spend most of your waking hour with your colleagues, so make an effort to develop a strong, friendly relationship with them. Watch movie with them or host a potluck dinner at your place.

Read at Least One Book a Month

Warren Buffet reads at least 500 pages a day. Bill Gates reads 50 books a year and Mark Zuckerberg reads two books a month. It's quite obvious that ultra-successful people are great readers.

Reading doesn't only make you smarter; it also reduces stress and improves your concentration. It's also a great past time.

Do the Things That Make You Happy

Life is too short. Don't spend every waking hour in your office. Get a hobby. Do something you love. Spend time gardening, hiking, bike riding, writing, dancing, and painting. Do something that makes your heart sing.

Be a Good Team Player

Don't be arrogant. You can't achieve great things alone, no matter how good you are. So, learn to embrace teamwork.

Teamwork improves your patience. It also helps you teaches you to stay confident despite of your weakness and be humble despite of your achievements.

Don't Rush

You'll eventually feel anxious if you're always in a rush. Take things slow. Eat as slowly as you can. Enjoy the flavors of your food. Drink your coffee as slowly as you can.

Don't Work Too Hard

Hard work is great. It's the key to success. But, too much hard work can cause fatigue. So, take time to relax. Take a break when you need it.

Try Breakfast in Bed

There's nothing more romantic than having breakfast in bed. So, try eating breakfast in bed with your partner every now and then.

Avoid Stress When You Can

Stress is deadly. It can kill you, so avoid it when you can. Don't work too much and leave work on time.

Remember that when you're in your death bed, you won't think about those days when you stayed in the office. You'll think about the days you spent with your loved ones.

CHAPTER 6

Hygge Minimalism: Get Cozy without Creating Clutter

Minimalism is the art of living with less. It is the art of giving up anything that's inessential. Like hygge, it has become popular and it has become a tool used to achieve peace, clarity, and happiness.

Living with less has a lot of benefits. It helps you save money and get rid of all the clutter around your house. It also increases your clarity, allowing you to focus on more important things. It brings more happiness, joy, and peace into your life. It helps you get out of debt and achieve financial independence, too.

But, can you practice hygge and minimalism at the same time? Can you get cozy without spending a lot of money and creating clutter? The answer is, of course, yes!

Here's a list of tips that you can use to practice hygge minimalism:

1. Donate or sell all the things that no longer sparks joy in your heart.

If that old coffee dresser is no longer making you happy, give it away or sell it on eBay. Get rid of things that are no longer cozy and comfortable. For example, if that old bag is no longer useful to you, hold it. Take time to appreciate everything it has done for you. Then, lovingly put it in a box and donate it to people who may need it.

2. Clear all the decorative clutter in your home.

Decorative items like paintings and figurines are great because they add color and personality to your home. But, too much décor can be distracting. So, to increase your mental clarity and peace, remove all the unnecessary decorative items in your home.

Use neutral colors when decorating your home. Avoid using too many colors. You can use wooden lampshades and tables, these items make your home feel warm and cozy. Invest in a few throw pillows and don't forget the candles. Use light and indoor plants as décor.

3. Buy less.

Both minimalism and hygge discourage excessive consumption. Buy only what you need. Invest in a few high quality clothes and items. When shopping for clothes, go with a few classic pieces that can stand the test of time like – a black dress, a brown trench coat, a few pairs of blue jeans, white shirts, black turtlenecks, and flesh summer dresses.

4. Keep your personal and work space organized.

Living in a cluttered home can be so stressful. Plus, it would probably take you 30 minutes to find a pen if you live in a messy home. This can be extremely frustrating.

So, to build a happy and peaceful life, you have to organize your home. Get rid of the things you no longer need and organize everything in your home. Put similar things in one drawer. Don't forget to label each drawer, cabinet, and containers. This way, it's easier for you to find things.

5. Use natural materials like wood, fresh flowers, and wools in decorating your home.

Décor made of natural materials are usually cheaper and they make your house feel cozy and homey, too.

6. Donate your magazines and unused books to hospital rooms.

Creating a book nook is one of the best ways to practice hygge. But, you should only keep the books and magazines that you like. If you own magazines and books that you are no longer interested in, give them to hospitals so people in the waiting room have something to read.

Gather the toys that your kids have outgrown and give them to a children's hospital or an orphanage.

7. Think before you buy.

Before you buy something, take time to think. Do you really need it? Can you afford it? Can it make your life happier and more peaceful?

8. Get rid of everything that's no longer working.

That unfixable electric fan is taking a lot of space and it's no longer making you happy. So, you've got to get rid of it.

9. Clean your home regularly.

As previously mentioned, messy homes are not homey and comfortable. That's totally the opposite of hygge. To make your home more cozy, you have to clean your house at least twice a week. You don't have to clean every part of your house, you can simply sweep your floors and wipe out the dust on the windows and tables.

10. Minimize your social media time.

Social media is good because it allows you to communicate with friends living in different parts of the world. But, it can also spark jealousy and can make you feel less of a human being. Looking at your friends' vacation photos can reduce your life satisfaction.

Spending too much time on social media can also make you feel alienated and disconnected. It can keep you from having "face to face" conversations. It can also keep you from building happy and fulfilling relationships.

Remember that less is always more. You don't have to splurge on expensive things to live a more comfortable life. You just have to have to get rid of things you don't need, invest in classic items, keep your home clean and organized, and surround yourself with things that make your heart skip a beat.

CHAPTER- 7

Hygge for Different Seasons

A lot of people think that hygge is only for winter. That's far from the truth. You can practice hygge for different seasons. You can use hygge to slow down during warmer months. You can also use it cozy up during colder months.

Winter Season

Winter is a magical time. It is that time of the year some cities turn into a snowy white wonderland. Everything seems sparkly.

But, the winter season can be cold, gloomy, and sometimes depressing. So, you have to make an extra effort to make your home look cozy, homey, warm, and comfortable.

Here's a list of hygge tips that you can use to cozy up during the coldest days of the year:

1. Drink hot chocolate in the morning.

2. Invest in a soft and high quality blanket.

3. Light scented candles around the house.

4. Invite friends over. Being with the people you love keeps your heart warm during those cold winter days.

5. Watch your favorite TV shows with people you love.

6. Read a good book by the fireplace.

7. Set the table.

8. Play some good vibes music around the house.

9. Wear warm socks. Keep your feet warm at all times.

10. Eat warm soup at night.

11. Wear flannel shirts. It's also a good idea to invest in a few luxurious cashmere sweaters.

WINTER HYGGE RECIPES

These recipes are warm, delicious, and taste a little bit like sunshine. So, unleash your inner chef and start cooking these delectable dishes.

Broccoli Cheddar Soup

This wonderful soup keeps you warm during cold winter nights. It has a rich flavor and it's packed with nutrients, too. This recipe is good for people.

Ingredients:

- ¼ cup of flour
- ¼ cup of melted butter
- 2 cups of cream (half and half)
- 1 cup of sliced broccoli
- 2 cups of chicken stock
- ¼ teaspoon of ground nutmeg
- 1 cup of julienned carrots

- Salt and pepper, as needed
- 1 cup of shredded cheddar cheese
- ½ cup of chopped onion

Direction:

Place one tablespoon of melted butter in a pan over medium heat and saute the onions for a few seconds. Add the rest of the melted butter and slowly add the "half and half" cream. Add the chicken stock and let the mixture simmer for 5 minutes.

Add the carrots and broccoli and cook for twenty minutes. Add the nutmeg, salt, pepper, and cheddar cheese. Cook until the cheese melts. Remove from the heat and serve with garlic bread.

Scandinavian Pork Belly with Parsley Sauce

This classic dish has a little bit of a "kick". It's sinful, tasty, and perfect for winter dinner parties.

Ingredients:

- 1 kilo boneless pork belly (cut into one inch slices)
- 2 cups of boiled potatoes, peeled and sliced
- Salt and pepper, as necessary
- 1 tablespoon olive oil
- 2 cups of milk
- ½ cup of melted butter

- ½ cup of finely chopped parsley

- ¼ cup of plain flour

Directions:

Preheat the oven to 200 degree Celsius. Season the pork with salt and pepper. Brush the pork with oil. Place the pork in a roasting tray and cook for 40 minutes. Remove from the oven and place it on a plate with potatoes.

Place the butter in a saucepan over medium heat. Add the flour. Stir constantly. Add the milk, salt, pepper, and parsley. Simmer for 30 seconds.

Pour the sauce over the pork and potatoes. Serve hot.

Ginger Latte

Ginger has strong anti-inflammatory properties. It strengthens your immune system and it also calms your spirit.

Ingredients:

- ½ cup of hot water
- ¼ teaspoon of ground ginger
- ½ cup of milk
- 2 teaspoons of maple syrup

Direction:

Combine all ingredients in a large mug. Stir well until it's smooth and creamy. Serve hot with cookies or cinnamon bread.

Lavender Latte

This winter drink has a soothing effect. It's delicious and has that rich taste that makes you feel like home.

Ingredients:

- 2 1/2 cups of milk
- ½ teaspoon of dried lavender flowers
- 2 teaspoon of instant coffee
- 3 tablespoons of sugar or other sweetener

Directions:

Heat the milk and lavender in a saucepan. Let the mixture simmer for one minute. Remove from the heat and drain the lavender from the coffee.

Add the sugar and the instant coffee. Pour the mixture into two mugs. Serve with your favorite snack.

Caramel Apple Pancake

This pie has American roots, but it's just as "hygge" as cinnamon bread. This dessert has a rich flavor. It sparks a bit of joy in your heart. It makes you feel good, too.

Ingredients:

- 3 large eggs
- ¾ cup of whole milk
- Kosher salt, as needed
- 1 teaspoon of vanilla extract
- 3 tablespoon of butter
- ½ teaspoon of ground cinnamon
- 3 tablespoons of white sugar
- 3 apples, sliced

Directions:

Preheat the oven to 400 degrees Fahrenheit. Process the eggs and milk in the blender. Add the vanilla, flour, cinnamon, a pinch of salt, and lemon zest. Blend again for 15 minutes. Set aside.

Melt the butter in an oven-safe skillet over medium heat. Add the sugar and apples. Reduce the heat. Stir constantly and cook for 25 minutes. Pour the egg mixture over the apples.

Place the pan in the oven and bake the cake for 20 minutes. Serve hot.

Swedish Almond Cake

This cake is tender, soft, and makes you feel good. It's perfect for the holidays.

Ingredients:

- ¼ cup of ground almonds
- 1 teaspoon of almond extract
- 2 beaten eggs
- ½ cup of softened butter
- 1 cup of all-purpose flour
- 1 cup of white sugar

Directions:

Preheat the oven to 350 degrees Fahrenheit. Combine the sugar, eggs, flour, and butter in a large bowl.

Grease the pie plate with butter. Pour the flour mixture. Add the almond extract and ground almond on top. Bake the pie for 25 minutes. Remove from heat and cut into 16 wedges.

AUTUMN

Autumn looks glorious with all its colors. It's that time of the year when the leaves turn to red, yellow, orange, and sometimes, purple. It's not too hot and not too cold, either. It's the perfect time of the year to just walk around and enjoy all the wonders this world has to offer.

Here's a list of hygge tips that you can use during the autumn season:

1. Use a cashmere scarf. It makes you feel cozy and super comfortable.

2. Drink a cup of cocoa, milk, tea, or soup. Make sure to put your hands around the cup before you take a sip. This will help you feel warm and cozy.

3. Host a game night and invite your closest friends. You can play board games together or you can play your favorite Xbox game.

4. Light some tealight candles in the bathroom while you're taking a bath. This will make you feel a little bit special and a bit warm, too.

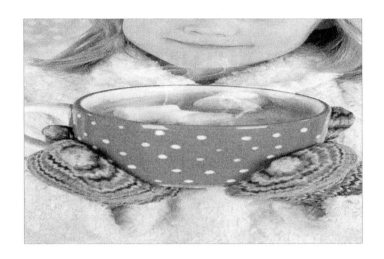

5. You don't have to spend a lot of money on a scarf. You can knit one.

6. Walk around your neighborhood in the late afternoon and watch the sunset.

7. Drink hot water with lemon. This is not only delicious. It also helps boost your metabolism.

8. Place soft blankets on the sofa so you could wrap yourself up while watching your favorite TV show.

9. Create a hygge corner that's decorated with throw pillows and good books.

10. Don't work too much. Try to come home as early as you can and spend a lot of time with your family and friends.

AUTUMN RECIPES

Autumn is one of the most beautiful seasons. You could see warm hues of red, yellow, orange, and green. It's just breathtaking.

French Onion Soup Casserole

This French dish is a popular European comfort food. It's cheesy and extremely satisfying. It's perfect for those cold autumn days.

Ingredients:

- 3 sliced onions
- 3 tablespoons of melted butter
- 4 cups of beef broth
- ½ cup of grated parmesan cheese
- 1 cup of shredded mozzarella cheese
- One loaf of French baguette bread (toast and slice into 12 small pieces)

- 1 tablespoon of Worcestershire sauce

Directions:

Heat the butter in a saucepan. Add the onions. Cover the pan and cook for 10 minutes. Add the Worcestershire sauce and broth. Cook for another 15 minutes under low heat.

Pour the broth mixture in a greased casserole dish. Add the toasted bread slices and then top with mozzarella and Parmesan cheese.

Bake for 10 to 20 minutes.

Slow Cooker Swedish Meatballs

This is a Swedish dish that has a rich taste. It is perfect for dinner parties.

Ingredients:

- 1 ½ teaspoons of ground allspice
- 2 eggs
- ½ cup of breadcrumbs

- 1 cup of ground turkey

- 1 cup of ground beef

- 1 tablespoon of Worcestershire sauce

- 1 cup of beef broth

- 1 teaspoon of onion powder

- ¼ cup of sour cream

- ½ cup of chopped parsley

- 3 tablespoons of all-purpose flour

- Salt and pepper, as needed

- 1 cup of beef broth

Directions:

Place the Worcestershire sauce and broth in a bowl. Add the eggs, bread crumbs, beef, onion powder, turkey, salt, and pepper. Mix well and roll the mixture into balls.

Place the meatballs in a slow cooker. Cook for two hours.

While waiting, combine the butter and flour in a medium-sized bowl. Mix well. Add the sour cream.

Add the sour cream sauce to the meatballs and cook in the slow cooker for another 30 minutes. Serve hot.

Kava Chai

Kava root increases mental clarity. It also reduces stress and anxiety.

Ingredients:

- 3 tablespoons of ground kava root

- 1 can of coconut milk

- ¼ teaspoon of vanilla extract

- 1 teaspoon of cardamom

- 3 tablespoons of sliced ginger root

- ½ teaspoon of ground cinnamon

- 3 cups of water

- 3 tablespoons of maple syrup

Direction:

Place 3 cups of water in a pan over medium heat. Add the vanilla extract, cardamom, ginger root, kava root, and cinnamon. Remove from the heat and refrigerate the mixture overnight.

In the morning, reheat the mixture and add the coconut milk. Add the maple syrup. Remove from heat and serve with cookies.

Caramel Mocha Drink

This drink contains melted Nutella. It surely tastes like heaven.

Ingredients:

- Whipped cream, as needed

- ½ cup of caramel sauce

- 3 tablespoons of instant coffee

- ¼ cup of cocoa powder

- ½ cup of melted Nutella

- 8 cups of "half and half"

Direction:

Place the half and half, melted Nutella, cocoa powder, instant coffee, and caramel sauce in a slow cooker. Cover and cook for four hours.

Pour the mixture in four tall glasses. Top with whipped cream.

Cinnamon Coffee Cake

This delicious cake is synonymous "hygge". It's perfect for cool autumn days.

Ingredients:

For the cake

- 1 ½ cups of milk
- ¼ teaspoon of salt
- 4 tablespoons of baking powder
- 2 teaspoons of vanilla
- 3 cups of flour
- 1 cup of sugar
- 2 eggs
- ½ cup of melted butter

Glaze

- 1 teaspoon of vanilla
- 2 cups of powdered sugar
- 5 tablespoons of milk

Topping

- 1 tablespoon of cinnamon
- 2 tablespoons of flour
- 1 cup of brown sugar
- 1 cup of melted butter

Directions:

Preheat the oven to 350 degrees Fahrenheit. Mix all the cake ingredients in a large bowl – 1 ½ cups of milk, two eggs, salt, baking powder, sugar, melted butter, and vanilla. Mix well. Set aside.

To make the topping, combine the cinnamon, flour, melted butter, and brown sugar in a large bowl. Set aside.

Pour the cake mixture into a greased 9 x 13 pan. Pour the cake mix in the pan. Swirl with a knife. Then, pour the topping mix. Bake for 30 minutes.

While waiting, combine the glazing ingredients in a small bowl.

Remove the baking pan from the oven and pour the glazing mixture on top of the cake. Serve with your favorite drink.

Cinnamon Walnut Energy Bars

This amazing dish is perfect for autumn dinner parties. It's sweet and gives you a lot of energy, too.

Ingredients:

- 1 cup of chopped walnuts
- 2 tablespoons of water
- 1 teaspoon of vanilla extract
- 2 tablespoons of mayonnaise
- 1 cup of confectioners' sugar
- ¼ teaspoon of salt
- 1 teaspoon of ground cinnamon
- 1 teaspoon of baking soda
- 2 cups of flour
- 1 egg
- ¼ cup of organic honey
- ¾ cup of vegetable oil (canola or olive)
- 1 cup of regular white sugar

Directions:

Preheat the oven to 350 degrees Fahrenheit. Combine the chopped walnuts, salt, cinnamon, baking soda, egg, flour, honey, sugar, and vegetable oil.

Grease a baking pan and pour the mixture into it. Bake for 10 minutes.

While waiting, mix the vanilla, water, mayonnaise, and confectioners' sugar. Remove the pan from the oven and pour the mayonnaise mixture on top. Let the cake set for 15 minutes, then cut into bars.

SPRING

Spring is the time when flowers bloom. It's the time to go out with friends, enjoy the beautiful outdoors, and just admire nature's wonders.

Many people think you don't need hygge in the spring. But, remember that hygge is something that you can practice all year round in every part of the world.

Here's a list of tips that you can use to practice hygge during springtime:

1. Let the natural light in.

2. Declutter your home and get rid of all your extra stuff.

3. Light floral scented candles. You can try rose, gardenia, and ylang ylang.

4. Prepare tasty desserts.

5. Host a potluck dinner party and invite your neighbors and friends.

6. Place fresh flowers around your house.

7. Jog in the morning and enjoy the mild heat of early morning sunshine.

8. Serve fresh salads.

9. Visit national parks and enjoy the great outdoors.

10. Plant trees with your friends. This is a good bonding activity. The future generation will also thank you for this.

SPRING RECIPES

Greek Roasted Lamb

This Greek dish is better shared with your friends. It's so good that it feels a little bit like home.

Ingredients:

- 1 kilo of boiled potatoes, peeled, salted, and sliced into half
- 1 cup of baby kalamata olives
- 6 tablespoons of olive oil
- ¼ cup of lemon juice
- ½ cup of oregano leaves
- 6 garlic cloves
- 1 large leg of lamb
- Salt and pepper

Directions:

Heat the oven to 240 degrees Celsius. Place the olive oil, lemon juice, garlic cloves, and olive oils in a food processor. Blend for 30 minutes.

Stab the lamb six times and place the lemon mixture into the holes. Season the lamb with salt and pepper. Roast the lamb for thirty to forty five minutes.

Serve the lamb with olives and potatoes. This dish is good for 7 to 8 people.

Crustless Bacon Quiche

This quiche is sinful, tasty, and powerful enough to evoke feelings of joy and satisfaction.

Ingredients:

- 1 cup of cubed cooked bacon
- 1 cup of cubed ham
- 1 cup of chopped broccoli
- 1 cup of cubed potato
- 6 eggs

- 1 cup of milk

- 1/2 cup of shredded Parmesan cheese

- 1 cup of shredded cheddar cheese

- Salt and pepper, as needed

Directions:

Preheat the oven to 350 degrees. Place all ingredients in a large bowl. Mix well. Pour the mixture into a greased pie pan. Bake for 30 to 40 minutes.

Creamy Blueberry Cake

This blueberry cake tastes a lot like spring. There's something about this creamy cake that can put you in a good mood.

Ingredients:

- 30 crushed wafers

- 2 cups of frozen blueberries

- 1 pack of lemon instant pudding mix

- 4 eggs

- 1 cup of sour cream

- 2 tablespoons of flour

- 4 packs of softened cream cheese

- 3 tablespoons of melted butter

- 1 cup and 3 teaspoons of white sugar

Directions:

Heat the oven to 325 degrees Fahrenheit. Combine the wafers, three teaspoons of sugar, and butter in a bowl. Press the mixture into a pan and bake for ten minutes.

While waiting, combine one cup of sugar, flour, and cream cheese in a mixer. Stir in the eggs, sour cream, pudding mix and 1 cup of blueberries.

Place the cream cheese mixture on top of the wafer crust. Put the pain in the oven again and bake for 40 minutes.

Remove the pan from the oven. Let it cool for a few minutes. Place the remaining blueberries on top of the cake and refrigerate for at least four hours before serving.

Oreo Mousse

This cold dessert is classic and will keep you asking for more.

Ingredients:

- A handful of mixed berries

- 1 cup of whipped topping

- 10 Oreo, crushed

- 2 cups of milk

- 1 pack of instant pudding mix

Directions:

Whisk the milk and pudding mix in a bowl. Add the crushed Oreos. Mix well.

Place the mixture int0 4 small glasses. Top with whipped topping and mixed berries. Refrigerate for at least two hours before serving.

Carrot and Orange Juice

This refreshing drink is perfect for warm spring days. It can also do wonders to your health.

Ingredients:

- 1 cup of ice
- 8 peeled oranges
- 2 large carrots, chopped and peeled

Directions:

Place the carrots and oranges in a juicer. Pour the juice into a large glass and add ice.

Beet Apple Drink

This refreshing drink is not only delicious, it's healthy, too.

Ingredients:

- 2 beets, peeled and chopped
- 3 carrots, peeled and chopped
- 1 green apple, sliced and seeded
- 2 cups of water

Directions:

Combine all ingredients in a blender. Blend for one minute.

Pour into two glasses and add ice.

SUMMER

Many people think that hygge is not necessary during summertime. But, you can create hygge moments during sunny days, too. Remember that hygge is not just about keeping yourself warm, it's about being happy. It's about being grateful and connected. It's about enjoying all the great things this life has to offer.

Here's a list tips that you can use to practice hygge during the summer:

1. Host a backyard barbecue party with your family and friends.

2. Play outdoor sports. This produces a cocktail of "feel good" hormones in your brain.

3. Spend time on the beach and enjoy the warm weather.

4. Use leafy plants as décor. It gives your home a warm, tropical vibe.

5. Place faux fur on your sofa to make it more comfortable.

6. Put fresh peonies in a mason jar and place it on your kitchen table.

7. Use soft cotton blankets.

8. Place shells in your living room. It gives you house that beach vibe.

9. Stargaze with your spouse or loved one.

10. Watch the sunset every single day.

SUMMER RECIPES

Tropical Fruit Water

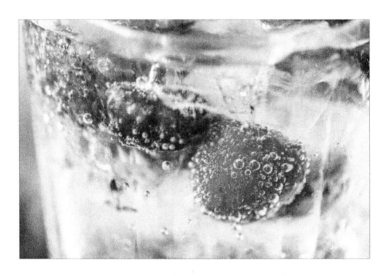

Summer days can get so hot, so you have to stay hydrated. This infused water is cool, delicious, and most of all, healthy.

Ingredients:

- A handful of mint
- ¼ cup of raspeberries
- ¼ cup of sliced blackberry
- ¼ cup of sliced and peeled kiwi
- ½ cucumber, sliced

- Distilled water
- Ice

Directions:

Place all the ingredients in a pitcher. Refrigerate for at least four hours before serving.

Ube Shake

This drink is served in "Jeepney" restaurant in New York City. It's sinful and perfect for the summer.

Ingredients:

- 6 ice cubes
- 1 tablespoon of rum
- 1 cup of milk
- 1 tablespoon of ube jam
- 2 scoops of ube ice cream

Directions:

Combine all the ingredients in a blender. Process until it's smooth. Pour the mixture in a milkshake glass. Serve and enjoy.

Creamy Pesto Pasta

This dish makes you feel cozy and comfy during summer. It's a classic, too.

Ingredients:

- 1 pack of penne pasta (450 grams) cooked according to package instructions
- 1 cup of cheddar cheese
- 2 cups of cream
- ¼ cup of olive oil
- 1 cup of basil leaves
- Salt and pepper
- 1 cup of chopped ham

Directions:

Place the basil leaves and the olive oil in the blender. Blend for a few minutes. Set aside.

Place a little bit of olive oil in a saucepan over medium heat. Add the chopped ham and cook for about 2 minutes. Add the basil leaves mixture. Simmer for five minutes and stir in the cream. Add salt and pepper. Stir well and add the cooked pasta.

Classic Macaroni Salad

This classic recipe is perfect for summer. It's a great source of carbohydrates. And you don't need to have strong culinary prowess to make this delicious dish.

Ingredients:

- 450 grams of macaroni
- 1 cup of mayonnaise
- 1 cup of "half and half"
- 2 tablespoons of chopped pimento peppers
- 1 cup of cheese
- 1 cup of shredded cooked chicken
- Salt and pepper, as needed

Directions:

Cook the macaroni according to package instructions. Place the cooked macaroni in a bowl.

Add all the mayonnaise and "half and half". Mix well. Stir in the cooked chicken and peppers. Add the salt, pepper, and cheese. Serve with toasted garlic bread.

Fresh Fruit Salad

This fruit salad is not only delicious. It's packed with vitamins and minerals.

Ingredients:

- ½ cup of raspberries
- ½ cup of green grapes
- 2 pieces of kiwi fruit, peeled and cut into small pieces
- ½ cup of strawberries, chopped
- Sweetened cream, as needed

Directions:

Combine all the fruits in a large bowl. Divide the mixture into four cups. Refrigerate for at least two hours. Drizzle with sweetened cream before serving.

Mango Sød

This tropical dessert has a little bit of Danish twist.

Ingredients:

- ½ cup of crushed Graham crackers
- 1 mango, thinly sliced
- ½ cup of condensed milk
- ½ cup of cream

Directions:

Combine the cream and condensed milk in a bowl. Set aside.

Place a layer of crushed Graham crackers in a dessert glass.

Then, place a layer of the condensed milk and mango strips.

Repeat this process until the dessert glass is full.

Refrigerate this dessert for four hours before serving.

CHAPTER- 8

Classic Hygge Recipes

Good food brings joy. It nourishes your body and spirit. It gives you a natural high and instantly puts you in a good mood.

Good food is very much a part of the hygge practice. Below are the recipes that you can prepare for yourself, your friends, and family no matter where you are in the world.

Scandinavian Comfort Food Recipes

Comfort foods relax and calm you. They make you feel at home and helps reduce stress. Below are two of the most delicious Scandinavian comfort foods.

Danish Mac and Cheese

Every American kid likes Mac and Cheese, but this comfort food has a Danish twist. This contains ramson, which is commonly found in many Nordic dishes. This recipe is perfect for any season. It makes you feel giddy, warm, and happy!

Ingredients:

- 1 cup of shredded cheddar cheese
- A handful of finely chopped ramson leaves
- ½ teaspoon of black pepper powder
- ¼ cup of butter
- 1/4 cup of cold milk
- 1 cup of macaroni (cooked according to instructions)
- 2 tablespoon of tapioca starch
- A dash of salt

Directions:

Heat a small skillet. Add the butter and stir until it's melted. Add the milk, ransom, and the tapioca starch. Add the macaroni pasta and stir well. Season the mixture with pepper and salt.

Remove the mixture from the skillet and transfer to a baking dish. Bake for 5 to 10 minutes (or until the cheese melts). Serve with garlic bread.

Flæskesteg

Flæskesteg is the ultimate Danish food and it's usually served during Christmas dinner. But, you can cook this tasty pork dish for an ordinary get-together with your family and friends.

Ingredients:

- 5 pound pork tenderloin
- Dried cloves
- Salt and pepper

- Dried bay leaves

Directions:

Preheat the oven to 450 degree Fahrenheit. Pat the pork and cut ½ inch incisions halfway down the fatty area.

Combine 2 tablespoon of salt with cloves, and pepper. Insert the bay leaves into the cut and the, rub the salt mixture all over the tenderloin.

Place the pork in a roasting pan and roast for thirty minutes. Remove the pan from the oven and pour three cups of boiling water into the roasting pan. This will make the pork crispy.

Place the pan back in the oven. Lower the temperature to 350 degrees and cook for one hour.

Let the pork rest for at least ten minutes in the oven before serving. Serve with mashed or buttered potatoes.

HYGGE DRINKS

If you want to surround yourself with happiness, you have to

Glögg: **Cozy Mulled Wine**

This spiced wine can cheer you up during cold and gloomy windy days. It has a fantastic aroma that will put you in good mood. This Swedish recipe has been passed down to several generations since 1921.

Ingredients:

- 1 liter of dry red wine
- 2 cinnamon sticks (cut into half so you'll have four sticks)
- 1 orange rind
- 1 lemon rind
- 4 tablespoons of sugar
- 1 teaspoon of whole cloves

- 1 teaspoon of allspice

Directions:

Combine the cinnamon, cloves, allspice, rind, and red wine in a saucepan over medium heat. Stir in the sugar. Keep stirring until it's dissolved. Cook for 20 minutes.

Remove from heat and pour into four glasses.

White Chocolate with Whipped Cream

This amazing hot drink can instantly put you in a good mood. It's sweet and perfect for every season. There's something about this drink that sparks a little bit of joy in your heart.

Ingredients:

- Whipped cream, as needed
- 1 cup of white chocolate chips
- 2 cups of whole milk
- 1 tablespoon of vanilla extract

Directions:

Mix the chocolate chips, whole milk, and vanilla extract over medium heat. Mix well until the mixture is smooth.

Pour the hot chocolate into two cups. Serve with bread or cookies.

HYGGE DESSERTS

Gingerbread Cake with Lingonberries

This cake is perfect for rainy days because it tastes a lot like sunshine. Plus, this cake has lingonberry which can prevent cancer. These berries also have a cocktail of vitamins and minerals, such as fiber, vitamin A, vitamin C, and magnesium.

Photo Source: canadianfamily.com

Ingredients:

- ½ cup of lime juice

- 50 grams of lingonberries

- 400 grams of sifted icing sugar

- 1 ½ cup of cream cheese

- 1 ½ cup of softened butter

- 2 cups of whole milk

- ½ teaspoon of vanilla extract

- ½ teaspoon of ground cardamom

- 1 teaspoon of ground cloves

- 1 teaspoon of ground ginger

- 2 teaspoons of ground cinnamon

- 2 teaspoons of baking powder

- 300 grams of plain flour

- ¼ cup of ligh brown sugar

- 1 cup of caster sugar

- 3 eggs

- 2 cups of melted butter

Directions:

To make the icing, beat the icing sugar, cream cheese, and butter in a mixer. Whisk until smooth. Add the lime juice and the berries. Add a little bit of lingonberry juice to give the icing a pastel pink color. Set aside.

Beat the eggs, brown sugar, and caster sugar in a mixer. Mix until it's smooth and a bit fluffy. Set aside.

Combine the flour, baking powder, cinnamon, cloves, ginger, and cardamom in a bowl. Mix well. Then, pour the flour mixture into the egg mixture. Add a pinch of salt. Then, stir in the butter, vanilla, and milk.

Heat the oven to 180 degree Celsius. Grease three cake pans with line with parchment paper.

Pour the mixture into three round cake pans. Bake for 15 minutes. Remove the cake from the oven. Allow the cakes to cool for a few minutes.

Place one cake on your serving dish. Spread a layer of icing on top. Repeat this process with the 2nd and 3rd layers.

Place a generous amount of lingonberries on top of the cake. Serve with iced tea or tea.

Blueberry Yogurt Cake

This cake is rich in antioxidants. It's so good that it takes a little bit of heaven.

Ingredients:

- 2 cups of blueberries
- 1 cup of Greek yogurt
- 3 egg whites

- 3 egg yolks

- 1 lemon zest

- ½ cup of maple syrup

- 100 grams of butter

- ½ teaspoon of sea salt

- ½ teaspoon of ground vanilla

- ½ cup of rice flour

- 1 cup of almond flour

- 1 cup of rolled flour

- 2 cups of mixed berries

- 1 cup of regular yogurt

- 2 cups of whipped cream

Directions:

Preheat the oven to 350 degree Fahrenheit. Place the oats, butter, lemon zest, and maple syrup in the food processor and process for 30 seconds. Put the mixture in a huge bowl and add the rice flour, almond flour, vanilla, sea salt, and baking powder.

Add Greek yogurt and egg yolks. Beat for one minute. Add the egg whites and mix well.

Line the cake with parchment paper. Pour the cake mix into the pan. Bake the cake for 50 minutes. Remove the cake from the oven.

Combine whipped cream and regular yogurt. Cover the cake with the whipped cream mixture and top with mixed berries. You can also decorate the cake with fresh flowers. Serve with fruit juice or tea.

CHAPTER- 9

20 Healthy Hygge Foods That Will Make Your Heart Leap

Hygge is about enjoying simple pleasures. It is about enjoying good food. But, you don't have to eat greasy comfort foods to cozy up. Here's a list of healthy "hygge foods" that you can try:

Smørrebrød

This is a Danish open-faced sandwich. This treat is usually topped with smoked fish, beets, and cabbage. It is usually served with pumpkin soup.

Hot Smoked Salmon

This Scandinavian dish is a great source of protein. It's delicious and it has this rich flavor that almost tastes like love. This dish has interesting ingredients like sockeye salmon fillets, ground coriander seed, juniper berries, maple syrup, sugar, and oranges.

Lentil Soup

This soup keeps you warm during cold times. It contains vitamins and minerals that help reduce the risk of heart disease.

Pumpkin Mac and Cheese

This dish tastes like the classic "mac and cheese", but with a healthy twist. This comfort food is rich in vitamin A. It's low in calories and contains a cocktail of minerals, such as copper, potassium, protein, vitamin C, vitamin E, Iron, and vitamin B2.

Coconut Breakfast Porridge

This porridge is warm and tastes a little bit of summer. This dish contains vitamin B6, minerals, magnesium, manganese, and copper.

Vegan Pumpkin Cinnamon Rolls

Cinnamon roll is probably the most "hygge" dish. But, the regular cinnamon rolls are rich in calories.

This cinnamon roll dish contains a generous amount of pumpkin, which is rich in vitamin A.

Baked Rice Pudding

Danish people usually eat rice pudding during the holidays. This dish is creamy and it makes you feel giddy. It is easy to make, too.

Scalloped Vegan Potatoes

This dish is creamy and it's perfect for vegetarians. It is creamy and it has a rich taste and great for get-togethers.

Mushroom Soup

This soup is perfect for cold nights. It's creamy and it has a rich flavor that brings pleasure and joy to every part of your body. This dish has white wine, too. So, it has a little bit of kick. It's truly heartwarming.

Roasted Potatoes

This dish is nourishing and it has generous amounts of rosemary. It's fairly easy to make. This dish gives you enough energy to last through the day.

Nordic Pea Soup

This soup is served in many Scandinavian households. This soup is filled with folate, protein, fiber, phosphorous, manganese, and copper.

Spicy Kohlrabi Fries

This is healthier than the regular French fries, but it is just as delicious.

Spiced Hot Chocolate

Who says chocolate is not healthy? This drink is packed with antioxidants. It tastes good and makes you feel good, too.

This sweet drink is cozy and it's perfect for TV series marathon nights. It has a slightly different taste than the usual chocolate drink. It is easy to make, too. All you need to do is to mix a little bit of ground cinnamon, grated nutmeg, granulated sugar, ground ginger, chili powder, cardamom, milk, cocoa powder, and vanilla.

Saffron Risotto

This dish is usually served in December. It is beautiful and it is usually served during autumn. This cheesy dish has a rich taste and contains ingredients, such as squash, black pepper, Arborio rice, shallots, white wine, and cheese.

Creamy Cauliflower Soup with Roasted Chickpeas

This soup is tasty, yet healthy. It's a great source of fiber and contains nutrients and antioxidants. It makes you feel cozy. But, it also helps you lose weight.

Moroccan Lamb

As the name suggests, this dish comes from Morocco. It's exotic, spicy, and interesting. It exudes cosiness, pleasure, and comfort.

Matcha Latte

This drink is originally from Japan. And yet, it has a strong hygge vibe. It's powerful enough to melt all your stress away. It makes you feel warm and a little bit fuzzy. It also has a cancer-fighting ingredient called EGCG. It's beneficial for people with heart disease, cancer, and diabetes.

Chili

Chili is one of the most popular comfort foods. It contains capsaicin, which can lower one's blood pressure. It also contains lycopene, which is good for your heart.

Guacomole

Avocado is one of the most powerful super foods. It helps decrease your body fat and helps reduce your blood pressure. It's delicious, too. This dish is a great "hygge dish" during warm summer days.

Okra and Shrimp Gumbo

Shrimp can easily put you in a good mood. But, okra is the superstar in this dish. It's rich in dietary fiber. It reduces stress and it helps lower your cholesterol levels.

CHAPTER 10

Fifteen Days Hygge Challenge

Stephanie is a workaholic marketing director. She's good at what she does, but she's living an unbalanced life. She's often stressed and unhappy. One day, she had a nervous breakdown. She was so tired that she can't take it anymore. She locked herself inside a bathroom and she just can't stop screaming.

That's when she knew that she must change the way she lives. She checked a number of self-help blogs and came across with "hygge". She decided to give this Danish concept a try. She purchased a few candles, cozy blankets, and socks. She started to slow down. She started drinking tea and watching the sun rise every morning. She also decided to leave her work early and spend more time with her favorite people.

After two weeks, Stephanie started to feel happy and more relaxed. She's no longer stressed. She no longer sees the joy in working too much. Soon, hygge became part of her system. It became her way of life.

Like Stephanie, you can change your life by taking the fifteen day hygge challenge.

Day 1 – Tea Time

There's no better way to start your day than to have drink a hot cup of coffee. If it's winter time, you can have a cup of chamomile tea, sprinkled with a little ground cinnamon. You can sip the coffee by the fireplace so you'd feel warm.

Chamomile tea has a strong calming effect. It gives you that feeling of peace and joy. It reduces inflammation and it also decreases your blood sugar. It also strengthens your immune system and can even do wonders to your skin. It also reduces stress.

Cinnamon, on the other hand, has a cocktail of antioxidants. It reduces inflammation and helps control one's blood sugar.

If it's a warmer season, you can have a cup of green tea and sprinkle it with cinnamon. You can sit and drink the coffee in your patio or porch. Just relax and enjoy the beauty of your neighborhood.

Green tea is packed with antioxidants. It relaxes your body. Plus, it boosts your metabolism, too.

Day 2 – The Happiness List

Julie Andrews once sang "I simply remember my favourite things and then I don't feel so sad". Your thoughts affect your mood. If you spend your days thinking negative thoughts, you'll eventually get depressed.

But, if you think happy thoughts, you'll be in a good mood all day. So, sit down and list all the things that make you happy. It doesn't have to be grand. It can be as simple as a hot soup or it can be your partner.

Here's a list of happy things as a guide:

1. Bubble bath

2. Poodle

3. Warm chocolate drink

4. Soft sweater

5. Good music

6. Sandwich

7. Coffee breaks

8. Puppies

9. Cats

10. Cuddling

11. Laughter

12. Beautiful sandals

13. The smell of fresh flowers

14. A good book

15. Ice cream

16. A warm brownie cup

17. Hugs

18. Friends

19. Christmas

20. Family

Look at this list whenever you feel down and stressed. This will instantly spark joy in your soul.

Day 3 – Connect With People Around You

Enjoy a cup of hot chocolate in a cozy café. You can do this alone or you can do this with your friends.

Take time to spread warmth and happiness to the people around you. Ask the barista how he's doing and really listen to the answer. Spread joy wherever you go. Smile at strangers and spread good vibes. Use positive phrases and words throughout the day.

Here are a few "good vibes" phrases that you can use throughout the day:

1. Thank you. I really appreciate what you do for me.

2. You can do it. I believe in you.

3. You're almost there.

4. You are an amazing cook.

5. You look great today. I like what you did with your hair.

6. You've made it this far. Just keep going.

7. Thank you for your help.

8. I am proud of you.

9. You are awesome.

10. Good job! Your work is amazing.

Choose to say positive and uplifting words throughout the day. This will not only make you more likeable. It makes you happier, too.

Day 4 – Watch Your Favorite Movie with Your Loved Ones

You don't have to spend a lot of money to have fun with your loved ones. You can just do a simple viewing party in your home.

Ask your family and friends to come over your house. Prepare a warm drink and some chocolate cookies and watch your favorite movie with them. You can also watch positive, "feel good", and inspiring movies like "Forrest Gump", "The Bucket List", "Finding Nemo", "Up", "Willy Wonka & the Chocolate Factory", "The Proposal", "La Vita e Bella", and "The Greatest Showman".

Day 5 – Enjoy the Beauty of the Sunrise

There's something about the sunrise that's so captivating. The colors ignite joy in your soul. There's something magical about watching the sky change colors before your eyes.

So before you start your day, look out from your window or sit on your porch and watch the sun rise. This simple pleasure sparks happiness in your heart. The beauty of the sunrise reminds you that every day is a promise and that it's great to be alive.

Day 6 – Put Tealight Candles in Your Home

A tealight candle brings beauty in your homes. It creates a cozy atmosphere. It soothes and relaxes your spirit. Plus, it smells good, too.

Place your tealight candles on your dining table or in the living room. Use cardamom and berry scented candles if you want your home to smell like Christmas. You can use citrus-scented and lavender-scented candles to calm your spirit and feel more alive.

Day 7 – Cook Your Favorite Comfort Food

There's nothing more amazing than eating your comfort food on a bad day. So, play your favorite relaxing and "feel good" music and cook your favorite comfort food. Dance while you're preparing the ingredients. This will instantly lift your spirit and put you in a good mood.

Day 8 – Reap the Power of Hugs

Hugs are amazing. They reduce stress and create a cocktail of "feel good" hormones in your brain. They make you happier and helps melt all your fears. A hug feels like home.

So, take time to hug everyone you care about. Hug your spouse before he/she goes to work. Hug your kids before they go to school. Hug a friend who badly needs it. Hug your parents while you can.

Hugs make you happier. They melt away all your stress and worries. But, they also allow you to create deeper relationships with your friends and family.

Day 9 – Do Digital Detox

Social media is good when used in moderation. But, it's bad if your life revolves around it. Too much use of social media can cause depression and anxiety.

So, to rest peacefully, do a digital detox at night. Don't check your social media or use other electronic devices from 8 pm to 8 am. This 12 hour digital detox helps you connect more with your family and loved ones. It also makes you peaceful and allows you to live in the present moment.

Day 10 – Look at Old Photos

Old photos bring back happy memories. It transports you to a happy time where everything's happy and amazing. So, take a walk down the memory lane and look at your old photo albums. Be amazed with how good you look and how good life is.

Day 11 – Do Something You Loved To Do as a Child

To beat stress and live a happy life, you have to unleash your inner child. Do something you loved to do as a child – paint, dance, and sing. You must have the courage to pursue your childhood dreams. If you've always wanted to be a fashion entrepreneur, why not start selling bags on Amazon or any other online marketing platform?

Day 12 – Organize A Game Night

Game night is fun and exciting. It unleashes your playful side and helps you connect with the people you care about. It allows your inner child to come out and play, too.

So, host a game night and invite your family and closest friends. Send a text message, invite and prepare some snacks. You can serve pretzels, pizzas, chicken nuggets, spring rolls, pork skewers, chicken bites, zucchini fries, kale chips, or Greek yogurt muffins.

Day 13 – Read A Good Book

You know that reading is good for you. It helps you learn new things. It improves your concentration and inspires you to do great things. Most of all, it's relaxing. Reading transports you to a world of fantasies and possibilities.

So, pick a good book, sit in your book nook, and read for as long as you can (with your feet up). This reduces your anxiety and helps you fall asleep. Reading also boosts your happiness and increases your life satisfaction. It also pushes you to do whatever it takes to transform your dreams into a reality.

Here's a list of inspiring books read:

- ✓ You are a Badass: How to Stop Doubting Your Greatness and Start Living An Awesome Life by Jen Sincero

- ✓ Grit: The Power of Passion and Perseverance by Angela Duckworth

- ✓ Think and Grow Rich by Napoleon Hill

- ✓ The Subtle Art of Not Giving a F*ck: Counterintuitive Approach to Living A Good Life by Mark Manson

- ✓ The Courage to be Disliked by Fumitake Koga and Ichiro Kishimi

- ✓ Mindset: The New Psychology of Success by Carol S. Dweck

- ✓ The One Thing by Gary Keller

- ✓ The Secret by Rhonda Byrne

- ✓ The Alchemist by Paulo Coelho

- ✓ I Know Why I Caged Bird Sings by Maya Angelou

- ✓ Tuesday with Morrie by Mitch Albom

- ✓ The Great Gatsby by F. Scott Fitzgerald

- ✓ Harry Potter Books by J.K. Rowling

- ✓ The Life of Pi by Yann Martel

- ✓ The Perks of Being a Wallflower by Stephen Chbosky

- ✓ The Four Agreements by Don Miguel Ruiz

- ✓ The Happiness Project by Gretchen Rubin

- ✓ Eat Pray Love by Elizabeth Gilbert

These books will inspire you. They will make you want to honor your existing by pursuing your dreams.

Day 14 – Live in the Present Moment

Mindfulness (or the art of living in the present moment) can transform your life. It helps you enjoy the little things and let go of all your worries. It also helps you move past hurts, mistakes, and failure. It improves your creativity and it helps you appreciate your life more.

Here are a few tips that you can use to live in the present moment:

1. Appreciate your job and really enjoy it. It may not be your dream job, but it pays your bills.

2. Appreciate the different moments of the day. Embrace all the sounds, the sights, the smells, the sadness, and the happiness.

3. Forgive everyone who has hurt you in the past. Resentment can slowly destroy you. It can keep you from building a happy and fulfilling life. So, choose to forgive and move on from all the pain.

4. Eat like a food critic. Take time to appreciate the presentation of the dish – its appearance and colors. Take note of all the flavors you taste and eat as slowly as you can. This technique does not only increase your mindfulness. It also helps you lose weight.

5. Do not dwell on your past successes and accomplishments. Those are all on the past. Remember that if you are still talking about the things that you have done yesterday, it means that you have

not done much today. Don't waste your time thinking about your past glory and focus on what you can do today.

6. You can't appreciate the beauty of the present moment if you worry too much about the future.

7. Take time to stop and smell the flowers, literally.

8. When you feel overwhelmed or stressed, take a deep breath. Inhale through your mouth and exhale through your mouth. Appreciate how your chest goes up and down when you breathe as this makes you feel more alive.

9. When you take a shower, really feel the water touching your skin. Notice how smooth your skin is and how amazing the water makes you feel.

Living in the present moment makes you happier. It improves your concentration and it helps you appreciate all the beauty and happiness this life has to offer.

Day 15- Relax and Repeat

It takes at least 21 days to develop a habit and 90 days to adopt a lifestyle. So, just keep going. Take time to relax and take things slow. Drink a warm chocolate in the morning when it's winter or autumn. Drink a refreshing fruit juice on spring and summer mornings.

You can reap the magic of hygge no matter what season it is. Remember that hygge is not just about staying warm during the winter. It is about being cozy, being relaxed, and being connected with people who matter to you.

CONCLUSION

Thank you for downloading this book. I hope that this book can help you beat stress and adopt a more relaxed and cozy lifestyle.

Before you start your hygge journey, let's review the major points of this book:

- Hygge is a cozy Danish lifestyle. It is the art of enjoying the simple joys of life.

- This Danish concept help you keep warm during the cold winter days. But, you can practice it all year round. You can use this concept to stay cozy in hot summer and windy spring days.

- Surround your home with scented candles.

- Cook delicious comfort food. Invest in good books and soft blankets.

- Surround yourself with things that tell a story.

- Organize your home and let go of the things you no longer need.

- Just go with the flow.

- Try new hot drinks.

- Host a brunch and invite your family and friends.

- Read books that inspire you.

- Listen to happy music.

- Get more sun and enjoy the outdoors.

- Surround yourself with your tribe, people who believe in you.

- Tell your loved ones how much they mean to you.

- Try a winter sport.

- Go on an adventure with people you love.

- Practice hygge daily until it becomes part of who you are.

Hygge is not just a décor trend. It is a way of life. So, keep practicing all the techniques in this book until you master this ancient art of happiness.

I wish you the best of luck!

Printed in Great Britain
by Amazon

13383089R00079